W9-AYN-475

Greatest Love Songs of the '90s

Arranged for Easy Piano By Dan Coates

Project Manager: Carol Cuellar
Cover Design: Michael Ramsay
Cover Art: © Copyright 1998 PhotoDisc, Inc.

© 1999 WARNER BROS. PUBLICATIONS
All Rights Reserved

Any duplication, adaptation or arrangement of the compositions
contained in this collection requires the written consent of the Publisher.
No part of this book may be photocopied or reproduced in any way without permission.
Unauthorized uses are an infringement of the U.S. Copyright Act and are punishable by law.

Dan Coates

Photo: by Carin A. Baer

One of today's foremost personalities in the field of printed music, Dan Coates has been providing teachers and professional musicians with quality piano material since 1975. Equally adept in arranging for beginners or accomplished musicians, his Big Note, Easy Piano and Professional Touch arrangements have made a significant contribution to the industry.

Born in Syracuse, New York, Dan began to play piano at the age of four. By the time he was 15, he'd won a New York State competition for music composers. After high school graduation, he toured the United States, Canada and Europe as an arranger and pianist with the world-famous group Up With People.

Dan settled in Miami, Florida, where he studied piano with Ivan Davis at the University of Miami while playing professionally throughout southern Florida. To date, his performance credits include appearances on "Murphy Brown" and "My Sister Sam" and at the Opening Ceremonies of the 1984 Summer Olympics in Los Angeles. Dan has also accompanied such artists as Dusty Springfield and Charlotte Rae.

In 1982, Dan began his association with Warner Bros. Publications—an association that has produced more than four hundred Dan Coates books and sheets. Throughout the year, he conducts piano workshops nationwide, during which he demonstrates his popular arrangements.

Title	Artist	Pg.
ALL MY LIFE	K-CI AND JO JO	4
ALL THE MAN THAT I NEED	WHITNEY HOUSTON	14
ANGEL OF MINE	MONICA	9
AT THE BEGINNING	RICHARD MARX AND DONNA LEWIS	22
BECAUSE OF YOU	98°	18
BECAUSE YOU LOVED ME	CELINE DION	27
BY HEART	JIM BRICKMAN	32
DREAMING OF YOU	SELENA	40
FOR THE FIRST TIME	KENNY LOGGINS	35
FOR YOU I WILL	MONICA	48
FOREVER'S AS FAR AS I'LL GO	ALABAMA	52
FROM HERE TO ETERNITY	MICHAEL PETERSON	55
FROM THIS MOMENT ON	SHANIA TWAIN WITH BRYAN WHITE	66
HAVE YOU EVER REALLY LOVED A WOMAN?	BRYAN ADAMS	58
HOW DO I LIVE	LeANN RIMES	62
I BELIEVE IN YOU AND ME	WHITNEY HOUSTON	74
I CAN LOVE YOU LIKE THAT	JOHN MICHAEL MONTGOMERY	78
I CROSS MY HEART	GEORGE STRAIT	69
I DO	PAUL BRANDT	82
I DO (CHERISH YOU)	MARK WILLS	88
I DON'T WANT TO	TONI BRAXTON	85
I DON'T WANT TO MISS A THING	AEROSMITH	92
I FINALLY FOUND SOMEONE	BARBRA STREISAND AND BRYAN ADAMS	96
I SWEAR	JOHN MICHAEL MONTGOMERY	102
I WILL COME TO YOU	HANSON	106
I WILL REMEMBER YOU	SARAH McLACHLAN	114
I'LL NEVER BREAK YOUR HEART	BACKSTREET BOYS	110
I'M YOUR ANGEL	R. KELLY & CELINE DION	117
IF TOMORROW NEVER COMES	GARTH BROOKS	122
IF YOU EVER HAVE FOREVER IN MIND	VINCE GILL	125
IN THIS LIFE	COLLIN RAYE	128
KAREN'S THEME	RICHARD CARPENTER	131
THE KEEPER OF THE STARS	TRACY BYRD	134
KISSING YOU (LOVE THEME FROM "ROMEO + JULIET")	DES'REE	138
LOVE WILL KEEP US ALIVE	EAGLES	142
ME AND YOU	KENNY CHESNEY	146
MORE THAN WORDS	EXTREME	148
MY ONE TRUE FRIEND	BETTE MIDLER	153
NOW AND FOREVER	RICHARD MARX	166
OH HOW THE YEARS GO BY	VANESSA WILLIAMS	158
ONCE IN A LIFETIME	MICHAEL BOLTON	162
SOMETHING THAT WE DO	CLINT BLACK	169
TELL HIM	BARBRA STREISAND AND CELINE DION	174
TIME TO SAY GOODBYE	ANDREA BOCELLI	179
UN-BREAK MY HEART	TONI BRAXTON	184
UNTIL I FIND YOU AGAIN	RICHARD MARX	189
VALENTINE	JIM BRICKMAN	192
WHEREVER YOU GO	VOICES OF THEORY	196
YOU MEAN THE WORLD TO ME	TONI BRAXTON	202
YOU WERE MEANT FOR ME	JEWEL	208
YOU'RE STILL THE ONE	SHANIA TWAIN	213
YOUR LOVE AMAZES ME	MICHAEL ENGLISH	44

ALL MY LIFE

Words and Music by
RORY BENNETT and
JO JO HAILEY
Arranged by DAN COATES

© 1997 HEE BEE DOOINIT MUSIC/2 BIG PROD., INC./
EMI APRIL MUSIC INC. and JOEL HAILEY MUSIC
All Rights on behalf of HEE BEE DOOINIT MUSIC and 2 BIG PROD., INC.
Administered by WB MUSIC CORP.
All Rights Reserved

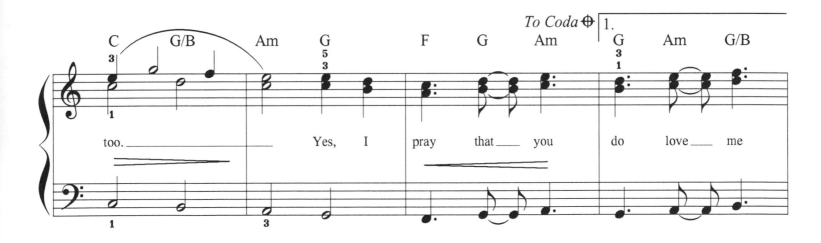

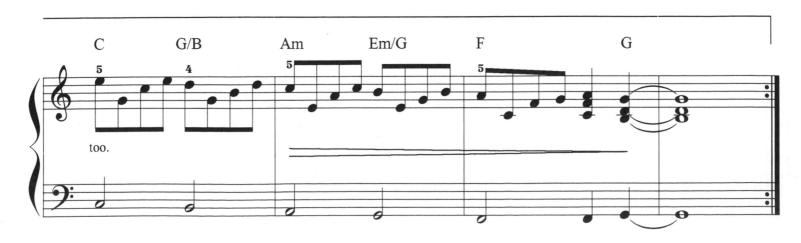

do love ___ me. You're all that ___ I ev - er know. ___ When you smile ___ on my face, ___ all I see ___

___ is a glow. ___ You turn my life ___ a - round, ___ you pick ___ me up when I ___ was

down. You're all that I ev - er know. When you smile, my face glows. You pick me up when I was

down. Say, you're all that I ev - er know. When you smile, my face glows. You pick me up when I was

Verse 2:
I promise to never fall in love with a stranger.
You're all I'm thinking of,
I praise the Lord above
For sending me your love.
I cherish every hug.
I really love you.
(To Chorus:)

ANGEL OF MINE

Words and Music by
RHETT LAWRENCE and TRAVON POTTS
Arranged by DAN COATES

Moderately slow ♩ = 96

G When I first saw you, I **A** al-read-y **Bm** knew

G there was some-thing **A** in-side of **Bm** you. **G** Some-thing I thought that I would

A nev-er **Bm** find, **A/C#** an-**D** gel **D/F#** of **G** mine.

Angel of Mine - 5 - 1

© 1998 WB MUSIC CORP., RHETTRHYME MUSIC and TRAVON MUSIC
All Rights on behalf of RHETTRHYME MUSIC Administered by WB MUSIC CORP.
All Rights Reserved

10

Angel of Mine - 5 - 3

12

ALL THE MAN THAT I NEED

Words and Music by
DEAN PITCHFORD and MICHAEL GORE
Arranged by DAN COATES

Slowly, with expression

All the Man That I Need - 4 - 1

© 1990, 1991 WARNER-TAMERLANE PUBLISHING CORP., BODY ELECTRIC MUSIC and FIFTH OF MARCH MUSIC
All Rights on behalf of BODY ELECTRIC MUSIC Administered by WARNER-TAMERLANE PUBLISHING CORP.
All Rights Reserved

BECAUSE OF YOU

Words and Music by
ANDERS BAGGE, ARNTHOR BIRGISSON,
CHRISTIAN KARLSSON and PATRICK TUCKER
Arranged by DAN COATES

Because of You - 4 - 1

© 1998 AIR CHRYSALIS SCANDINAVIA (AB)/MURLYN SONGS (STIM)
All Rights for AIR CHRYSALIS SCANDINAVIA (AB) in the US and Canada Administered by CHRYSALIS MUSIC (ASCAP)
All Rights Reserved   International Copyright Secured   Used by Permission

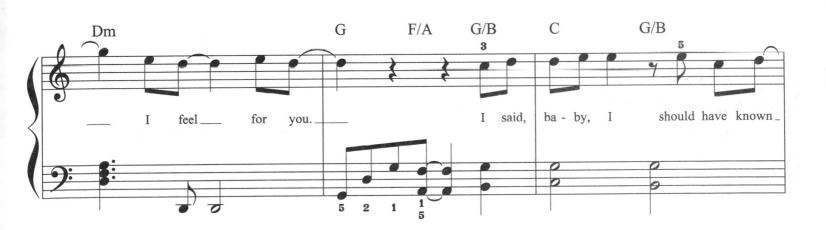

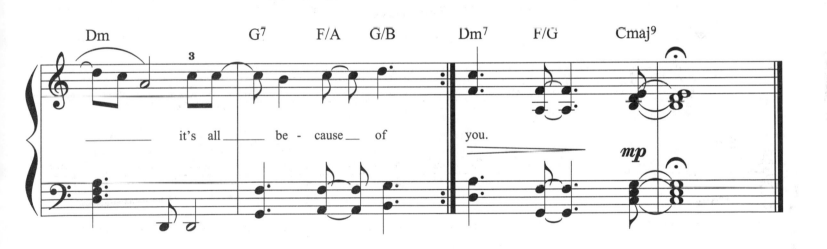

Verse 2:
Honestly, could it be you and me
Like it was before, need less or more?
'Cause when I close my eyes at night,
I realize that no one else
Could ever take your place.
I still can feel, and it's so real,
When you're touching me,
Kisses endlessly.
It's just a place in the sun
Where our love's begun.
I miss you,
Yes, I miss you.
(To Chorus:)

From the Twentieth Century Fox Motion Picture
"ANASTASIA"

AT THE BEGINNING

Lyrics by
LYNN AHRENS

Music by
STEPHEN FLAHERTY
Arranged by DAN COATES

Moderate rock ballad

© 1997 T C F MUSIC PUBLISHING, INC. (ASCAP)
This Arrangement © 1997 T C F MUSIC PUBLISHING, INC. (ASCAP)
All Rights Reserved

BECAUSE YOU LOVED ME
(Theme from "Up Close & Personal")

Words and Music by
DIANE WARREN
Arrnaged by DAN COATES

Because You Loved Me - 5 - 1

© 1996 REALSONGS (ASCAP)/TOUCHSTONE PICTURES SONGS & MUSIC INC. (ASCAP)
All Rights Reserved

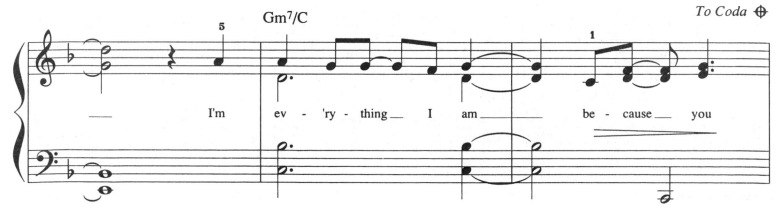

1.
F
B♭/C
loved me.
mp
2. You gave me
2.
F
A7
loved me.
mp
You were al - ways there
mf
Dm7
for me, the ten - der wind that car - ried me. A
A7
Dm
light in the dark, shin- ing your love in - to my life.

BY HEART

Composed by
JIM BRICKMAN and
HOLLYE LEVEN
Arranged by DAN COATES

By Heart - 3 - 1

© 1995 BRICKMAN ARRANGEMENT (SESAC) & SWIMMER MUSIC (SESAC) &
HOLLYE PENO MUSIC & POLYGRAM MUSIC PUBLISHING (BMI)
All Rights Reserved

By Heart - 3 - 2

By Heart - 3 - 3

From the Twentieth Century Fox Motion Picture "ONE FINE DAY"

FOR THE FIRST TIME

Words and Music by
JAMES NEWTON HOWARD,
ALLAN RICH and JUD FRIEDMAN
Arranged by DAN COATES

For the First Time - 5 - 1

© 1996 T C F MUSIC PUBLISHING, INC.,
SCHMOOGIE TUNES (Administered by PEERMUSIC LTD.),BIG FIG MUSIC (Administered by FAMOUS MUSIC CORP.)
and MUSIC CORPORATION OF AMERICA, INC./NELANA MUSIC (Administered by MUSIC CORPORATION OF AMERICA, INC.)
All Rights Reserved

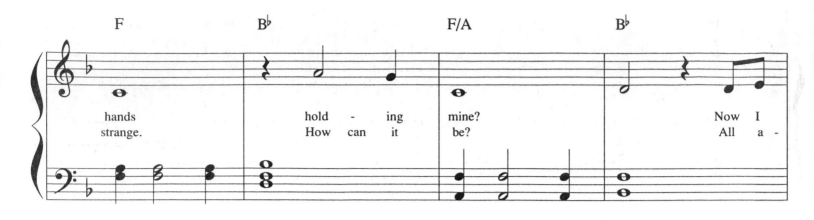

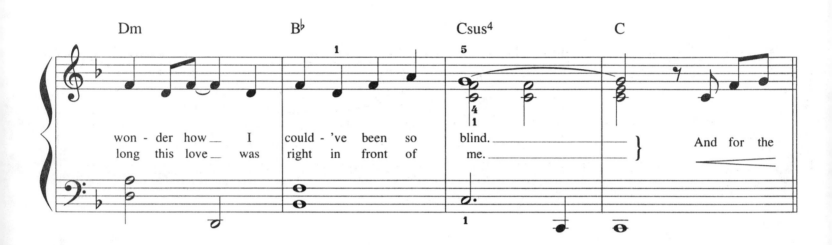

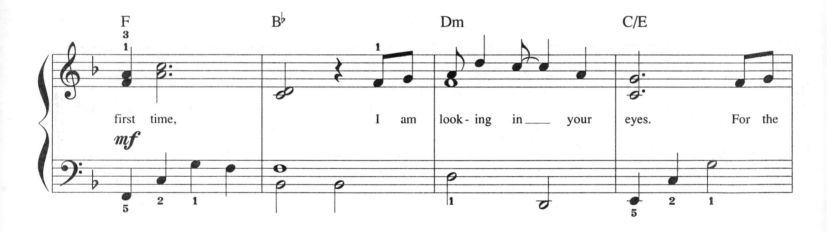

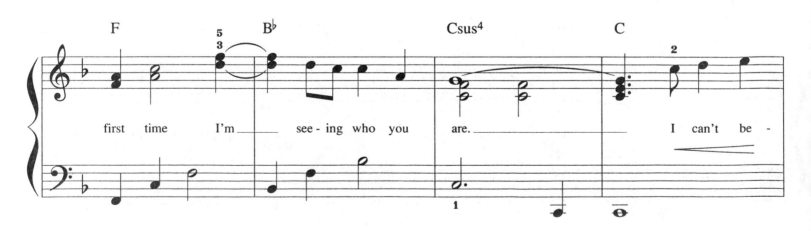

lieve how much ___ I see when you're look- ing back ___ at me. ___ Now I

un - der - stand what ___ love is, ___ love is ___ for the

dim.

first time. ___

mp

2. Can this be

2. Such a long time ___ a - go, ___ I had giv - en up ___ on

mf

first time, I'm ___ see - ing who you are. ___ I can't be -

lieve how much ___ I see when you're look- ing back __ at me. ___

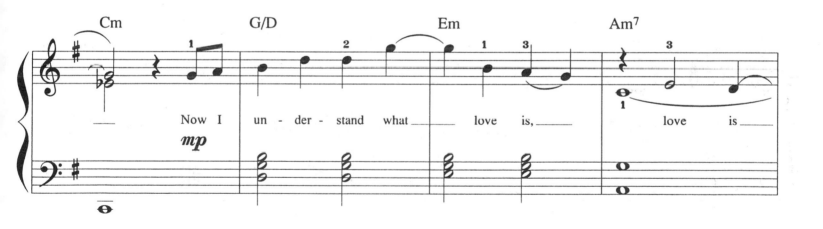

__ Now I un - der - stand what ___ love is, ___ love is ___

mp

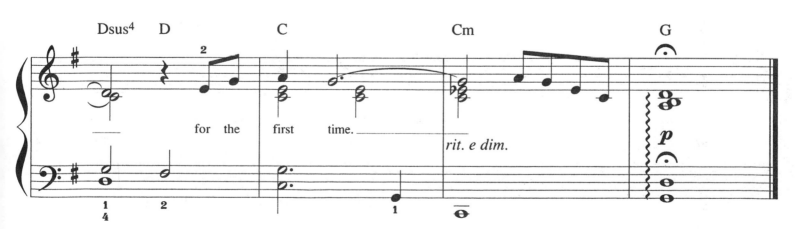

__ for the first time. ___

rit. e dim.

p

DREAMING OF YOU

Words and Music by
TOM SNOW and
FRAN GOLDE
Arranged by DAN COATES

Dreaming of You - 4 - 1

© 1989, 1995 SNOW MUSIC (ASCAP)/VIRGIN MUSIC, INC./CHESCA TUNES (BMI)
All Rights Reserved

42

YOUR LOVE AMAZES ME

Words and Music by
CHUCK JONES and AMANDA HUNT
Arranged by DAN COATES

Your Love Amazes Me - 4 - 1

© 1993 HAMSTEIN CUMBERLAND MUSIC (BMI)/DIAMOND STRUCK MUSIC (BMI)/ GILA MONSTER MUSIC (SESAC)
All Rights Reserved

But they ain't noth - in', ba - by, your love a - maz - es me.

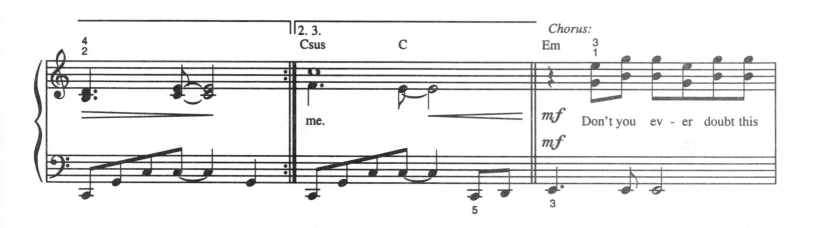

me. Don't you ev - er doubt this

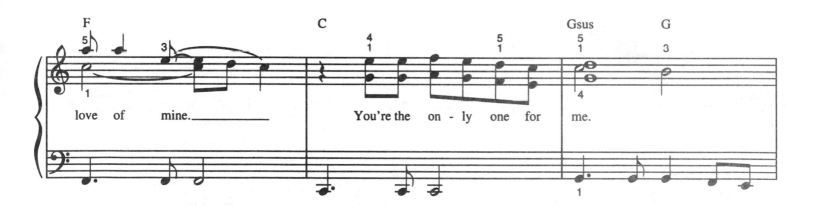

love of mine._____ You're the on - ly one for me.

You give me hope, you give me rea - son. You give me some - thing to be - lieve in.

46

For - ev - er faith - ful - ly, your love a - maz - es me.

Your love, your love,___

your love a - maz - es me.

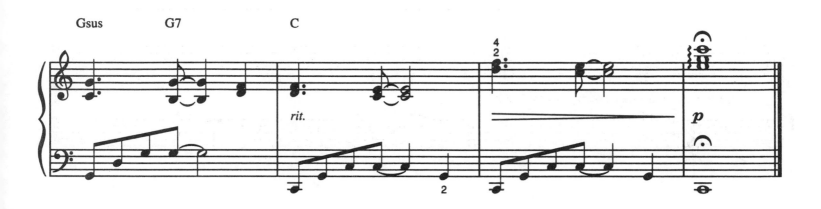

Verse 2:
I've seen a sunset that would make you cry,
And colors of a rainbow reaching 'cross the sky.
The moon in all its phases, but
Your love amazes me.
(To Chorus:)

Verse 3:
I've prayed for miracles that never came.
I got down on my knees in the pouring rain.
But only you could save me,
Your love amazes me.
(To Chorus:)

FOR YOU I WILL

Words and Music by
DIANE WARREN
Arranged by DAN COATES

Moderately slow ♩ = 72

Verse:

1. When you're feel - ing lost in the night, _____ when you feel your world just ain't right, _____ call on me, I will be wait - ing. Count on me, I will be there. An - y - time the times get too tough, _____ an - y - time your best ain't e - nough, _____ I'll be the one to make it bet - ter.

© 1996 REALSONGS/WB MUSIC CORP. (ASCAP)
All Rights Reserved

give my word, I'll give it all. Put your faith in me, I'll do an-y-thing. I will cross the

Coda will. Prom - ise you, for you I

will. I prom - ise you, for you I will.
rit. e dim.

Verse 2:
I will shield your heart from the rain,
I won't let no harm come your way.
Oh, these arms will be your shelter,
No, these arms won't let you down.
If there is a mountain to move,
I will move that mountain for you.
I'm here for you, I'm here forever.
I will be a fortress, tall and strong.
I'll keep you safe, I'll stand beside you,
Right or wrong.   *(To Chorus:)*

FOREVER'S AS FAR AS I'LL GO

Words and Music by
MIKE REID
Arranged by DAN COATES

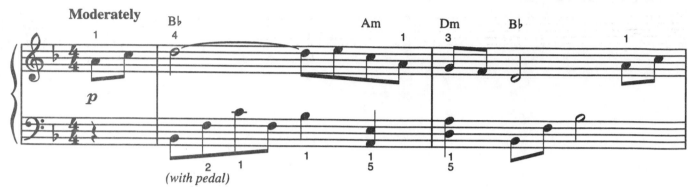

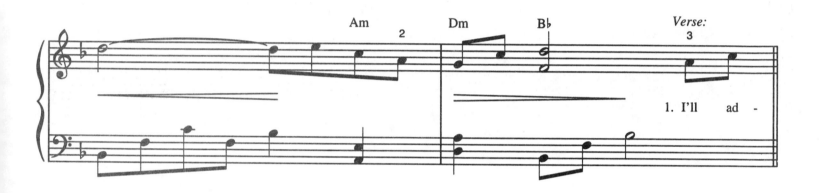

Forever's As Far As I'll Go - 3 - 1

Copyright © 1990 ALMO MUSIC CORP. and BRIO BLUES MUSIC (ASCAP)
International Copyright Secured   Made in U.S.A.   All Rights Reserved

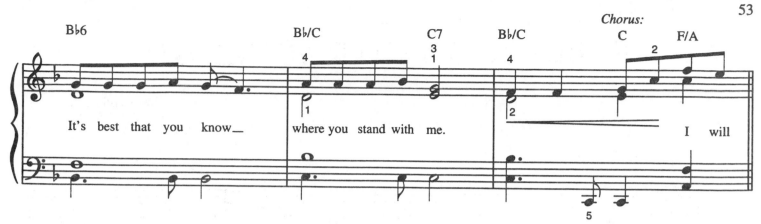

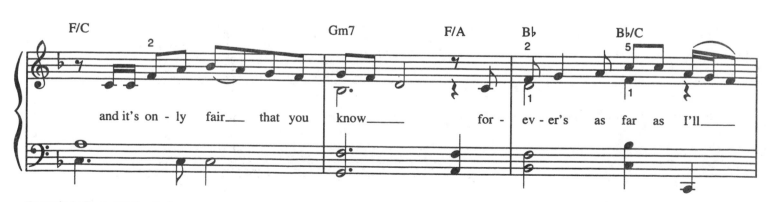

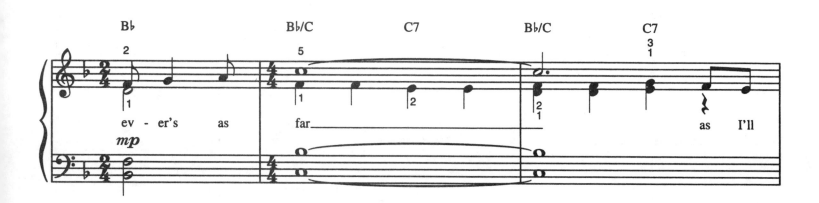

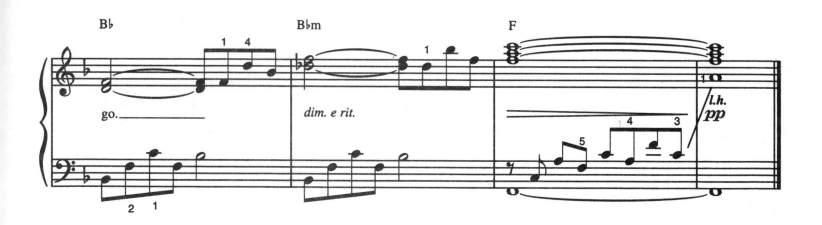

Verse 2:
When there's age around my eyes and gray in your hair,
And it only takes a touch to recall the love we've shared.
I won't take for granted that you know my love is true.
Each night in your arms, I will whisper to you...
(To Chorus:)

FROM HERE TO ETERNITY

Words and Music by
MICHAEL PETERSON and
ROBERT ELLIS ORRALL
Arranged by DAN COATES

From Here to Eternity - 3 - 1

© 1997 WARNER-TAMERLANE PUBLISHING CORP. (BMI)/EMI APRIL MUSIC INC./
JKIDS (Controlled and Adm. by EMI APRIL MUSIC INC.) (ASCAP)
All Rights Reserved

Verse 2:
I saved a year for this ring,
I can't wait to see how it looks on your hand.
I'll give you everything that one woman needs
From a one-woman man.
I'll be strong, I'll be tender, a man of my word.
And I will be yours...
(To Chorus:)

From the Original Motion Picture Soundtrack "DON JUAN DeMARCO"

HAVE YOU EVER REALLY LOVED A WOMAN?

Lyrics by
BRYAN ADAMS and
ROBERT JOHN "MUTT" LANGE

Music by
MICHAEL KAMEN
Arranged by DAN COATES

Have You Ever Really Loved a Woman? - 4 - 1

© 1995 BADAMS MUSIC LIMITED, OUT OF POCKET PRODUCTIONS LIMITED,
K-MAN MUSIC CORP., NEW LINE MUSIC CO. and SONY SONGS INC. (BMI)
All Rights on behalf of OUT OF POCKET PRODUCTIONS LIMITED
Controlled by ZOMBA ENTERPRISES INC. (ASCAP) for the U.S. and Canada
All Rights Reserved

59

Have You Ever Really Loved a Woman? - 4 - 2

HOW DO I LIVE

Words and Music by
DIANE WARREN
Arranged by DAN COATES

Moderately slow ♩ = 92

1. How do I get through one night with-out you?____ If I had to live with-out you,____ what kind of life would that be?____ Oh____ I,____ I need you in my arms, need you____ to hold. You're my

How Do I Live - 4 - 1

© 1997 REALSONGS (ASCAP)
All Rights Reserved

Verse 2:
Without you, there'd be no sun in my sky,
There would be no love in my life,
There'd be no world left for me.
And I, baby, I don't know what I would do,
I'd be lost if I lost you.
If you ever leave,
Baby, you would take away everything
Real in my life.
And tell me now...
(To Chorus:)

FROM THIS MOMENT ON

Words and Music by
SHANIA TWAIN and R.J. LANGE
Arranged by DAN COATES

From This Moment On - 3 - 1

© 1997 SONGS OF POLYGRAM INT'L INC./LOON ECHO INC. (BMI); OUT OF POCKET PRODUCTIONS LTD.
All Rights on behalf of OUT OF POCKET PRODUCTIONS LTD. Controlled by ZOMBA ENTERPRISES INC. (ASCAP) for the U.S. and Canada
All Rights Reserved   Used by Permission   International Copyright Secured

68

Verse 3:
From this moment, as long as I live,
I will love you, I promise you this.
There is nothing I wouldn't give,
From this moment on.

Chorus 2:
You're the reason I believe in love.
And you're the answer to my prayers from up above.
All we need is just the two of us.
My dreams came true
Because of you.

From the Warner Bros. Film "PURE COUNTRY"

I CROSS MY HEART

Words and Music by
STEVE DORFF and ERIC KAZ
Arranged by DAN COATES

I Cross My Heart - 5 - 1

© 1990, 1992 WARNERBUILT SONGS, INC., DORFF SONGS and ZENA MUSIC
All Rights on behalf of DORFF SONGS Administered by WARNERBUILT SONGS, INC.
All Rights Reserved

I Cross My Heart - 5 - 3

Additional Lyrics

2. You will always be the miracle
   That makes my life complete.
   And as long as there's a breath in me
   I'll make yours just as sweet.
   As we look into the future,
   It's as far as we can see.
   So let's make each tomorrow
   Be the best that it can be.
   (To Chorus)

From the Motion Picture "THE PREACHER'S WIFE"

I BELIEVE IN YOU AND ME

Words and Music by
SANDY LINZER and DAVID WOLFERT
Arranged by DAN COATES

© 1981, 1982 LINZER MUSIC COMPANY, CHARLES KOPPELMAN MUSIC,
MARTIN BANDIER MUSIC and JONATHAN THREE MUSIC
This Arrangement © 1997 LINZER MUSIC COMPANY, CHARLES KOPPELMAN MUSIC,
MARTIN BANDIER MUSIC and JONATHAN THREE MUSIC
All Rights Reserved

Verse 2:
I will never leave your side,
I will never hurt your pride.
When all the chips are down,
I will always be around
Just to be right where you are, my love.
Oh, I love you, boy.
I will never leave you out,
I will always let you in
To places no one has ever been.
Deep inside, can't you see?
I believe in you and me.

I CAN LOVE YOU LIKE THAT

Words and Music by
STEVE DIAMOND, MARIBETH DERRY
and JENNIFER KIMBALL
Arranged by DAN COATES

Moderately slow

(with pedal)

1. They read you Cin-der-el-la, you hoped it would come true, ___ that
nev-er make a pro-mise I don't in-tend to keep, ___ so

one day your Prince Charm-ing would come ___ res-cue you. ___ You
when I say for-ev-er, for-ev-er's what I mean.

like ro-man-tic mov-ies, you nev-er will for-get the way you felt when Ro-me-o kissed
I'm no Ca-sa-no-va, but I swear this much is true: I'll be hold-ing noth-ing back when

I Can Love You Like That - 4 - 1

© 1995 DIAMOND CUTS, CRITERION MUSIC CORP., WINDSWEPT PACIFIC ENTERTAINMENT CO., d/b/a FULL KEEL MUSIC CO.,
SECOND WAVE MUSIC and FRIENDS AND ANGELS MUSIC
All Rights in the U.S. and Canada Administered by WONDERLAND MUSIC COMPANY, INC.
All Rights on behalf of SECOND WAVE MUSIC and FRIENDS AND ANGELS MUSIC Administered by FULL KEEL MUSIC CO.
All Rights Reserved

I Can Love You Like That - 4 - 4

I DO

Words and Music by
PAUL BRANDT
Arranged by DAN COATES

© 1996 WARNER-TAMERLANE PUBLISHING CORP. and POLLYWOG MUSIC
All Rights Administered by WARNER-TAMERLANE PUBLISHING CORP.
All Rights Reserved

Verse 3:
I know the time will disappear,
But this love we're building on will always be here.
No way that this is sinking sand,
On this solid rock we'll stand forever.
(To Chorus:)

I DON'T WANT TO

Words and Music by
R. KELLY
Arranged by DAN COATES

© 1996 ZOMBA SONGS INC./R. KELLY PUBLISHING, INC. (Admin. by ZOMBA SONGS INC.) (BMI)
All Rights Reserved

I DO (CHERISH YOU)

Words and Music by
KEITH STEGALL and DAN HILL
Arranged by DAN COATES

© 1998 SMASH VEGAS MUSIC, a Division of BIG PICTURE ENTERTAINMENT (BMI)/
IF DREAMS HAD WINGS LTD. (ASCAP)
All Rights Reserved

yes, I do.

If you're

ask-ing do I love you this much,

I do,

oh, I do.

rit. e dim.

Verse 2:
In my world before you,
I lived outside my emotions.
Didn't know where I was going
Till that day I found you.
How you opened my life
To a new paradise.

In a world torn by change,
Still, with all of my heart
Till my dying day,
I do cherish you.   (To Chorus:)

From Touchstone Pictures' ARMAGEDDON

I DON'T WANT TO MISS A THING

Words and Music by
DIANE WARREN
Arranged by DAN COATES

© 1998 REALSONGS (ASCAP)
All Rights Reserved

I Don't Want to Miss a Thing - 4 - 4

From the Motion Picture "THE MIRROR HAS TWO FACES"

I FINALLY FOUND SOMEONE

Written by
BARBRA STREISAND, MARVIN HAMLISCH,
R. J. LANGE and BRYAN ADAMS
Arranged by DAN COATES

with pedal

simile

I fi - n'lly found some - one
that knocks me off of my feet.

I fi - n'lly found the one that
makes me feel com - plete.

I Finally Found Someone - 6 - 1

© 1996 OUT OF POCKET PRODUCTIONS LTD. (All Rights Controlled by ZOMBA ENTERPRISES INC. for the U.S. and Canada)/
BADAMS MUSIC LTD./EMANUEL MUSIC and TSP MUSIC, INC.
All Rights on behalf of BADAMS MUSIC LTD., EMANUEL MUSIC and TSP MUSIC, INC.
Administered by SONY/ATV MUSIC PUBLISHING, 8 Music Square West, Nashville, TN 37203
All Rights Reserved   Used by Permission

I Finally Found Someone - 6 - 5

I SWEAR

Words and Music by
GARY BAKER and FRANK MYERS
Arranged by DAN COATES

I see the ques - tion in your eyes,
I'll give you ev - 'ry-thing I can,

I know what's weigh - ing on your mind, but you can be sure
I'll build your dreams with these two hands, and we'll hang some mem-

© 1993, 1994 RICK HALL MUSIC, INC. and MORGANACTIVE SONGS, INC.
All Rights Reserved

I WILL COME TO YOU

Words and Music by
ISAAC HANSON, TAYLOR HANSON,
ZACHARY HANSON, BARRY MANN and CYNTHIA WEIL
Arranged by DAN COATES

When you have no light to guide you, and no one to walk be-side you, I will come to you, come to you.

When the night is dark and storm-y, you won't have to reach out for me. I will come to you, oh, come to you.

I Will Come to You - 4 - 1

© 1997 JAM 'N' BREAD MUSIC (ASCAP) and DYAD MUSIC LTD. (BMI)
All Rights on behalf of JAM 'N' BREAD MUSIC Administered by HEAVY HARMONY MUSIC
All Rights Reserved

night is dark and storm-y, you won't have to reach out for me. I will

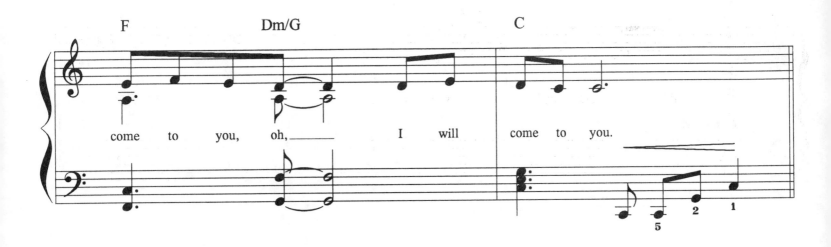

come to you, oh, _____ I will come to you.

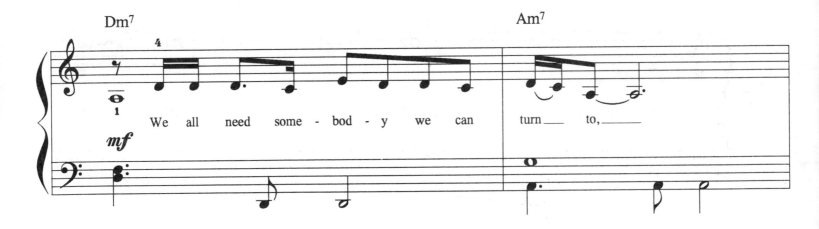

We all need some-bod-y we can turn ___ to, _____

some-one who'll al-ways ___ un-der- stand. _____

I'LL NEVER BREAK YOUR HEART

By
ALBERT MANNO and
EUGENE WILDE
Arranged by DAN COATES

© 1996 ZOMBA SONGS INC. and DUJUAN PUBLISHING
All Rights Administered by ZOMBA SONGS INC.
All Rights Reserved

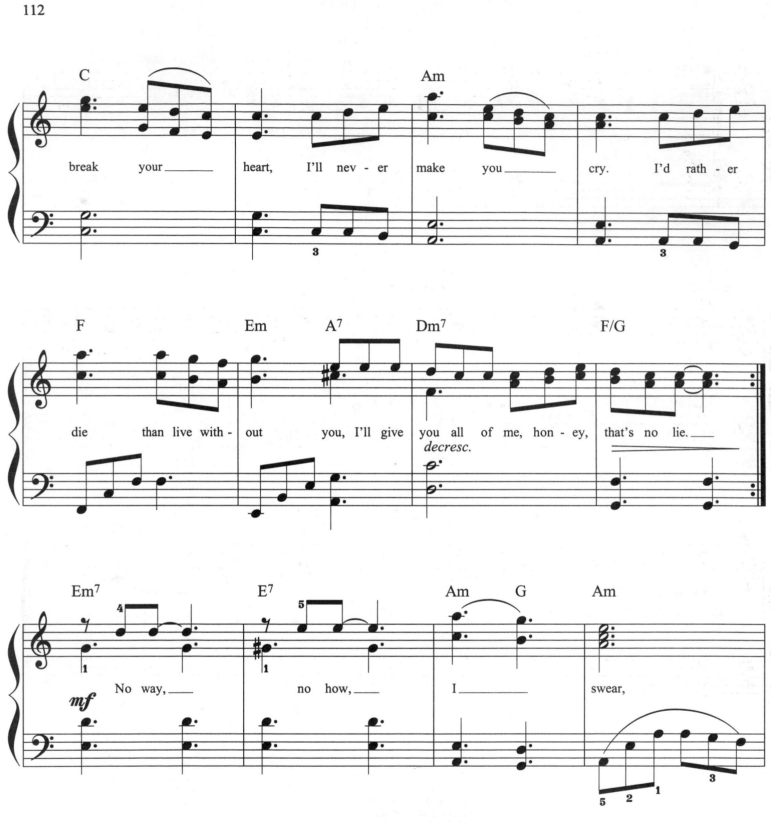

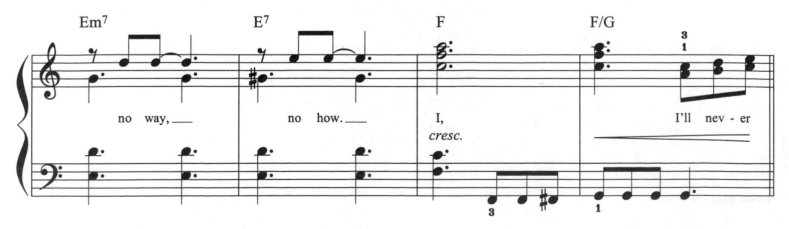

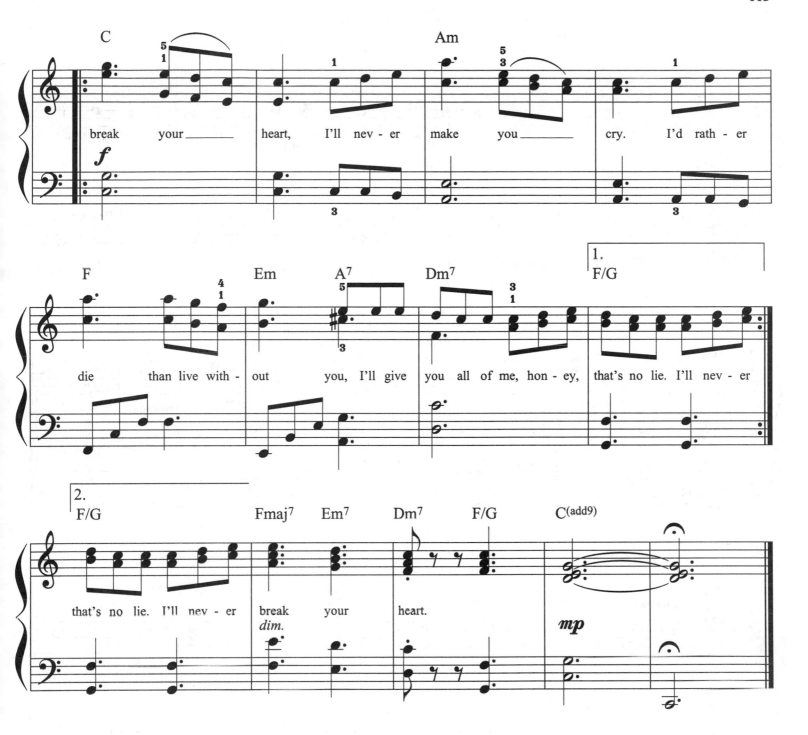

Verse 2:
As I walked by you,
Will you get to know me
A little more better?
Girl, that's the way love goes.
And I know you're afraid
To let your feelings show,
And I understand.
But girl, it's time to let go.
I deserve a try, honey,
Just once,
Give me a chance
And I'll prove this all wrong.
You walked in,
You were so quick to judge.
But, honey, he's nothing like me.
(To Chorus:)

From The Fox Searchlight Film, "THE BROTHERS McMULLEN"

I WILL REMEMBER YOU

Words and Music by
SARAH McLACHLAN, SEAMUS EGAN
and DAVID MERENDA
Arranged by DAN COATES

© 1995 T C F MUSIC PUBLISHING, INC., TYDE MUSIC, SEAMUS EGAN MUSIC and SONY SONGS, INC.
Rights on behalf of TYDE MUSIC Administered by SONY SONGS, INC.
Rights on behalf of SEAMUS EGAN MUSIC Administered by FOX FILM MUSIC DORP.
All Rights Reserved

I Will Remember You - 3 - 1

Verse 2:
So afraid to love you, more afraid to lose.
I'm clinging to a past that doesn't let me choose.
Where once there was a darkness, a deep and endless night,
You gave me everything you had, oh, you gave me life.
(To Chorus:)

I'M YOUR ANGEL

Words and Music by
R.KELLY
Arranged by DAN COATES

Moderately slow ♩ = 66

(with pedal)

1. No moun-tain's too high _____ for you to climb. _____ All _____ you have _____
2. I saw your tear-drops _____ and I heard you cry. _____ All _____ you need _____

_____ to do _____ is have _____ some climb - ing faith. _____
_____ is time. _____ Seek me and you _____ will find. _____

No riv-er's too wide _____ for you to make it a-cross. _____ All _____ you have _____
You have ev-'ry-thing _____ and you're still lone - ly. _____ It _____ don't have _____

I'm Your Angel - 5 - 1

© 1998 ZOMBA SONGS INC./R. KELLY PUBLISHING, INC.
All Rights on behalf of R. KELLY PUBLISHING, INC. Administered by ZOMBA SONGS INC. (BMI)
All Rights Reserved

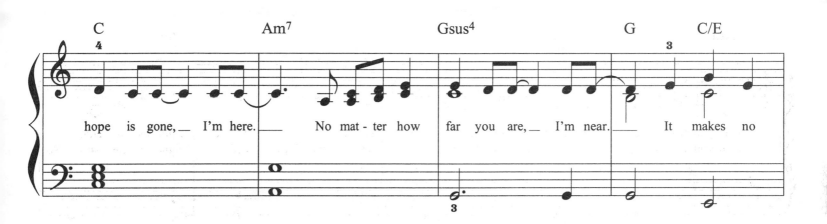

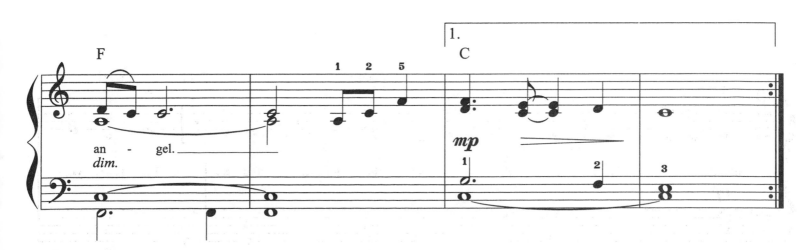

I'm Your Angel - 5 - 3

I'm Your Angel - 5 - 5

IF TOMORROW NEVER COMES

Words and Music by
KENT BLAZY and GARTH BROOKS
Arranged by DAN COATES

If Tomorrow Never Comes - 3 - 1

© 1988 EVANLEE MUSIC (ASCAP) and MAJOR BOB MUSIC CO., INC.(ASCAP)
All Rights Reserved

Verse 2:
'Cause I've lost loved ones in my life
Who never knew how much I loved them.
Now I live with the regret
That my true feelings for them never were revealed.
So I made a promise to myself
To say each day how much she means to me
And avoid the circumstance
Where there's no second chance
To tell her how I feel. 'Cause... *(To Chorus:)*

IF YOU EVER HAVE FOREVER IN MIND

Words and Music by
VINCE GILL and TROY SEALS
Arranged by DAN COATES

Slow country swing

If You Ever Have Forever in Mind - 3 - 1

© 1998 BENEFIT MUSIC/IRVING MUSIC, INC./BABY DUMPLIN' MUSIC (BMI)
All Rights Reserved

Verse 2:
Music has ended, still you wanna dance.
I know that feeling, I can't take the chance.
You live for the moment; no future, no past.
I may be a fool to live by the rules.
I want it to last.
(To Chorus:)

IN THIS LIFE

Words and Music by
MIKE REID and
ALLEN SHAMBLIN
Arranged by DAN COATES

Slowly ♩ = 72

(with pedal)

For all I'd been blessed with in my life,

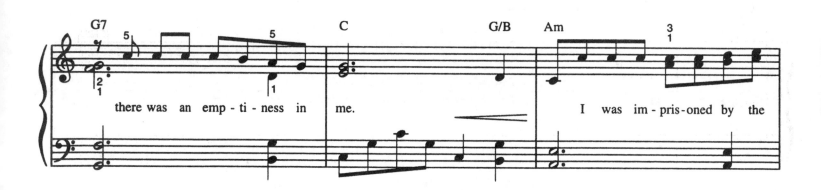

there was an emp-ti-ness in me. I was im-pris-oned by the

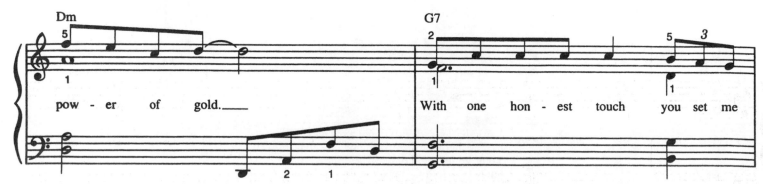

pow-er of gold.___ With one hon-est touch you set me

In This Life - 3 - 1

© 1992 ALMO MUSIC CORP./BRIO BLUES MUSIC (ASCAP)/HAYES STREET MUSIC/ALLEN SHAMBLIN MUSIC (ASCAP)
All Rights Reserved

free. Let the world stop turn-ing, let the

sun stop burn-ing. Let them tell me love's not worth___ go-ing

through. If it all falls a-part, I will

know deep in my heart the on-ly dream that mat-tered had come

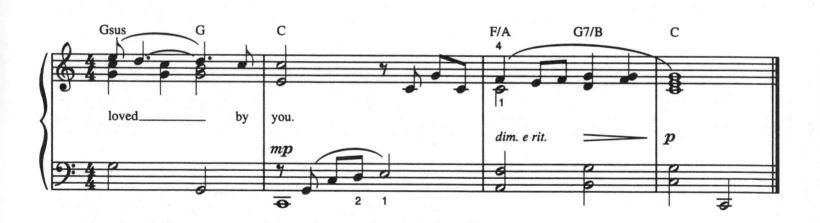

Verse 2:
For every mountain I have climbed,
Every raging river crossed,
You were the treasure that I longed to find.
Without your love I would be lost.
(To Chorus:)

KAREN'S THEME

Composed by
RICHARD CARPENTER
Arranged by DAN COATES

Slowly, with expression

Karen's Theme - 3 - 1

© 1998 ALMO MUSIC CORP. and HAMMER AND NAILS MUSIC (ASCAP)
All Rights Reserved

Karen's Theme - 3 - 3

THE KEEPER OF THE STARS

Words and Music by
KAREN STALEY, DANNY MAYO and DICKEY LEE
Arranged by DAN COATES

The Keeper of the Stars - 4 - 1

© 1994 NEW HAVEN MUSIC, INC., SIXTEEN STARS MUSIC,
MURRAH MUSIC CORPORATION, SONGS OF POLYGRAM INTERNATIONAL, INC. and PAL TIME MUSIC
All Rights Reserved

KISSING YOU
(Love Theme from "ROMEO + JULIET")

Words and Music by
DES'REE and TIM ATACK
Arranged by DAN COATES

© 1996 FOX FILM MUSIC CORP./SONY MUSIC PUBLISHING UK Admin. by SONY/ATV SONGS LLC (BMI)/
LOVE LANE MUSIC (UK) Admin. by WESTBURY MUSIC (PRS)
All Rights Reserved

LOVE WILL KEEP US ALIVE

Words and Music by
JIM CAPALDI, PETER VALE
and PAUL CARRACK
Arranged by DAN COATES

Love Will Keep Us Alive - 4 - 1

© 1994 FREEDOM SONGS LTD. (PRS), EMI VIRGIN MUSIC LTD. (PRS)
and PLANGENT VISIONS MUSIC LTD. (PRS)
All Rights on behalf of FREEDOM SONGS LTD. Administered by
WARNER-TAMERLANE PUBLISHING CORP. (BMI) in the U.S.A.
All Rights Reserved

ME AND YOU

Words and Music by
SKIP EWING and RAY HERNDON
Arranged by DAN COATES

© 1995 ACUFF-ROSE MUSIC, INC., (BMI) 65 Music Square West, NASHVILLE, TN 37203
SONGS OF RAYMAN, (BMI) 6846 E. Dreyfuss, Scottsdale, AZ. 85254
All Rights Reserved
The use of the lyrics of this song with any other music is expressly forbidden.

Verse 3:
Everyday I live,
Try my best to give
All I have to you.
Thank the stars above
That we share this love,
Me and you.

Verse 4:
Ordinary?
No, really don't think so.
Just a precious few
Ever make it last,
Get as lucky as
Me and you.

MORE THAN WORDS

Lyrics and Music by
BETTENCOURT, CHERONE
Arranged by DAN COATES

Moderate rock ballad ♩ = 92

Say - in' "I ___ love you" is not the words ___ I want to hear ___ from you. It's not that I ___ want you not to say, ___ but if you on - ly knew how ___

More Than Words - 5 - 1

© 1990 FUNKY METAL PUBLISHING (ASCAP)
All Rights Administered by ALMO MUSIC CORP. (ASCAP)
All Rights Reserved

Verse 2:
Now that I have tried to talk to you
And make you understand,
All you have to do is close your eyes
And just reach out your hands
And touch me, hold me close, don't ever let me go.
More than words is all I ever needed you to show.
Then you wouldn't have to say
That you love me, 'cause I'd already know.

MY ONE TRUE FRIEND

(From "ONE TRUE THING")

Words and Music by
CAROLE BAYER SAGER, CAROLE KING
and DAVID FOSTER
Arranged by DAN COATES

© 1998 ALL ABOUT ME MUSIC, LUSHMOLE MUSIC,
ONE FOUR THREE MUSIC, MUSIC CORPORATION OF AMERICA, INC.
and MCA MUSIC PUBLISHING, a division of MCA, INC.
All Rights on behalf of ALL ABOUT ME MUSIC Administered by WARNER-TAMERLANE PUBLISHING CORP.
All Rights Reserved

OH HOW THE YEARS GO BY

Words and Music by
WILL JENNINGS anf SIMON CLIMIE
Arranged by DAN COATES

Moderately slow ♩ = 88

p legato

Verse:

In our times of trou-ble,_____ we on-ly had our- selves,

no-bod-y else. No one there to save us,_____ we had to save our-

selves. And when the storms came through,_____ they found me and

© 1994, 1998 BLUE SKY RIDER SONGS (BMI) (Adm. by RONDOR MUSIC (LONDON) LTD.)/
SONY MUSIC PUBLISHING UK LTD./CLIMIE TO THE MOON MUSIC (ASCAP) (Adm. by SONY/ATV PUBLISHING)
All Rights Reserved

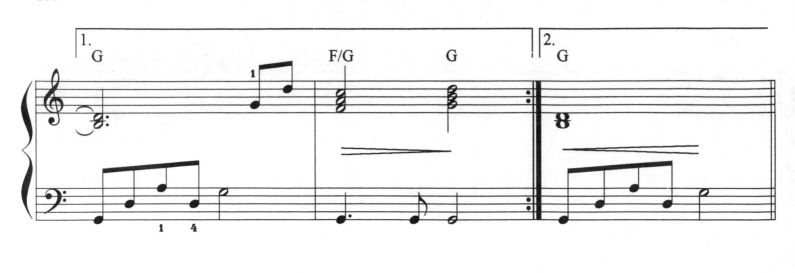

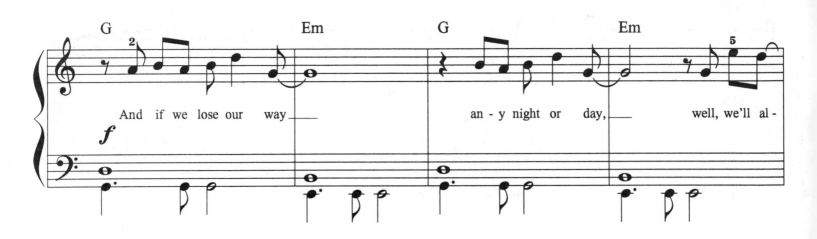

And if we lose our way ___ an - y night or day, ___ well, we'll al-

ways be ___ where we ___ should be. ___ I'm there ___ for you, ___ and I know ___

___ you're ___ there ___ for me. As the years go by. ___

Verse 2:
There were times we stumbled,
They thought they had us down,
We came around.
How we rolled and rambled,
We got lost and we got found.
Now we're back on solid ground.
We took everything
All our times would bring
In this world of danger.
'Cause when your heart is strong,
You know you're not alone
In this world of strangers.
(To Chorus:)

From the TriStar Pictures Feature Film "ONLY YOU"

ONCE IN A LIFETIME

Words and Music by
WALTER AFANASIEFF, MICHAEL BOLTON
and DIANE WARREN
Arranged by DAN COATES

Some peo-ple fill their lives with emp-ty nights and days that slip a-
Some peo-ple live their lives in com-pro-mise and hide their dreams a-

way. Some search till the end of time, but nev-er find the o-pen arms of
way. Some nev-er take the chance with-in their hands to claim the prize they

fate. One mo-ment comes a-long, and some-one hands your
make. When faith is all you need to hold the hand of

Once in a Lifetime - 4 - 1

© 1994 WB MUSIC CORP. (ASCAP), WALLYWORLD MUSIC (ASCAP),
MR. BOLTON'S MUSIC, INC. (BMI) and REALSONGS (ASCAP)
All Rights on behalf of WALLYWORLD MUSIC Administered by WB MUSIC CORP.
All Rights Reserved

NOW AND FOREVER

Music and Lyrics by
RICHARD MARX
Arranged by DAN COATES

© 1993 CHI-BOY MUSIC (ASCAP)
All Rights Reserved   Used by Permission

SOMETHING THAT WE DO

Words and Music by
CLINT BLACK and SKIP EWING
Arranged by DAN COATES

Something That We Do - 5 - 1

© 1997 BLACKENED MUSIC PUBLISHING (BMI)/ACUFF-ROSE MUSIC, INC. (BMI)
All Rights Reserved

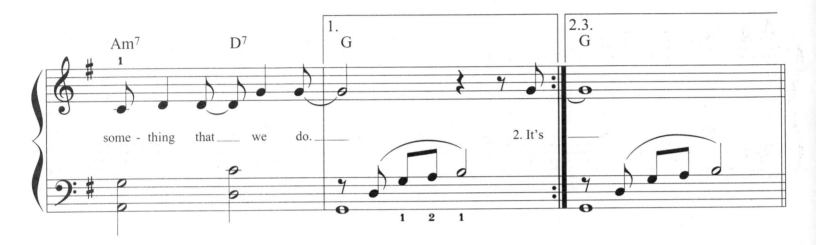

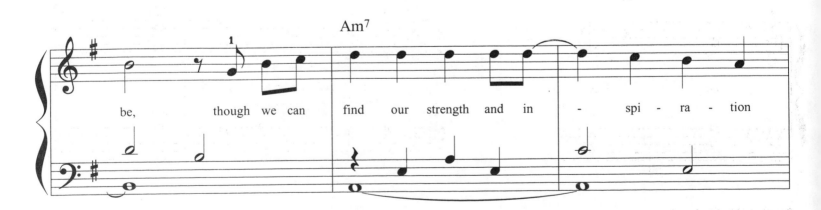

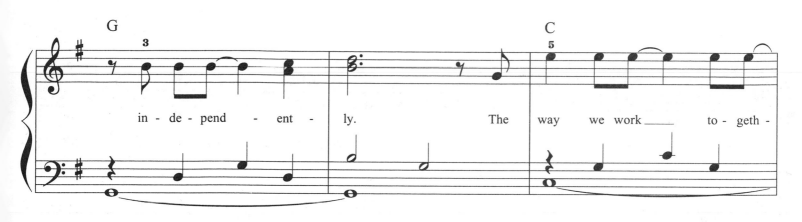

in - de - pend - - ent - ly.   The way we work _____ to - geth -

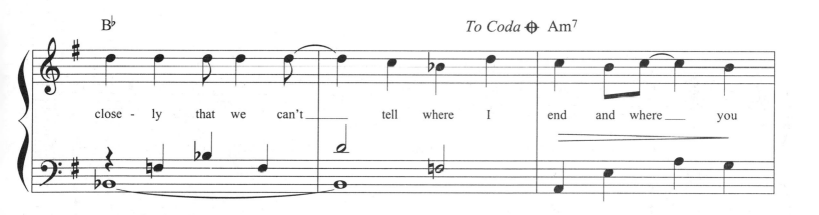

er is what   sets our love _____ a - part,   so

close - ly that we can't ___   tell where I   end and where ___ you

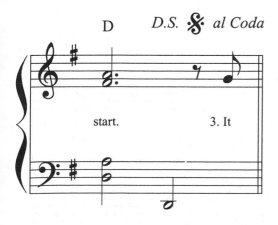

D.S. 𝄋 *al Coda*

start.   3. It

Coda ⊕ Am⁷   D

end and where ___ you   start.
rit.

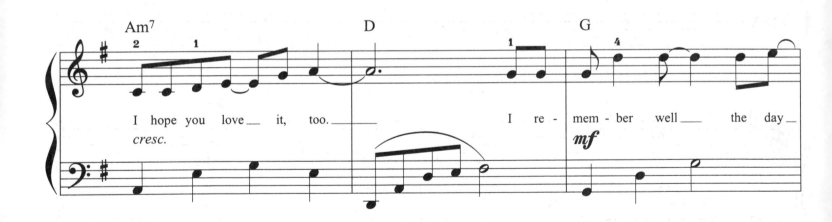

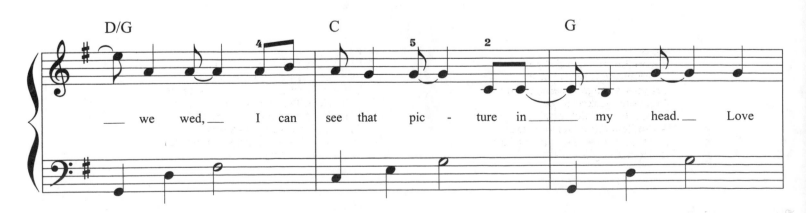

Verse 2:
It's holdin' tight, lettin' go,
It's flyin' high and layin' low.
Let your strongest feelings show
And your weakness, too.
It's a little and alot to ask,
An endless and a welcome task.
Love isn't something that we have,
It's something that we do.

Verse 3:
It gives me heart remembering
How we started with a simple vow.
There's so much to look back on now.
Still it feels brand new.
We're on a road that has no end,
And each day we begin again.
Love's not just something that we're in,
It's something that we do.

TELL HIM

Words and Music by
LINDA THOMPSON, DAVID FOSTER
and WALTER AFANASIEFF
Arranged by DAN COATES

Slowly ♩ = 76

Am

Celine:

1. I'm scared,

so a-fraid to show I care.

Em/G

Will he think me

weak

F

Dm

if I trem-ble when I speak?

C

E7

Am

What if

there's an-oth-er one he's think-ing of?

Em/G

© 1997 WARNER-TAMERLANE PUBLISHING CORP., BRANDON BRODY MUSIC,
ONE FOUR THREE MUSIC and WALLYWORLD MUSIC
All Rights on behalf of BRANDON BRODY MUSIC
Administered by WARNER-TAMERLANE PUBLISHING CORP.
All Rights Reserved

May-be he's in love. I'd feel like a fool. Life can be so

cruel. I don't know what to do. _____

Barbra:

I've been there, with my heart out in my hand.

But what you must un-der - stand, you can't let the chance to love him pass you

by. *Chorus: Both:* Tell _____ him,

tell him that the sun and moon rise in his eyes. Reach out to him _____ and

whis - per tender words so soft and sweet. I'll hold him close to feel his heart beat.

Love will be the gift you give your - self.

self. Love is light that sure - ly glows in the hearts of those who

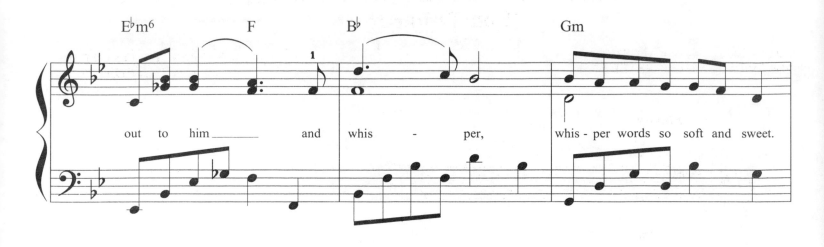

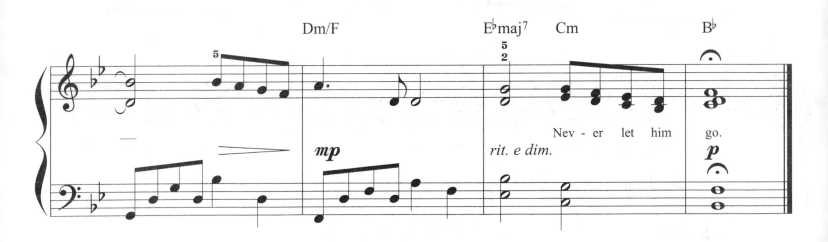

Verse 2:
(Barbra:)
Touch him with the gentleness you feel inside.
Your love can't be denied.
The truth will set you free.
You'll have what's meant to be.
All in time, you'll see.
(Celine:)
I love him,
Of that much I can be sure.
I don't think I could endure
If I let him walk away
When I have so much to say.
(To Chorus:)

TIME TO SAY GOODBYE
(Con Te Partiró)

Lyrics by LUCIO QUARANTOTTO
English Lyrics by FRANK PETERSON

Music by FRANCESCO SARTORI
Arranged by DAN COATES

Time to Say Goodbye - 5 - 1

© 1995 Insieme S.r.1. and Double Marpot Edizioni Musicali.
Controlled in the United States by Sugar-Melodi, Inc. and in Canada by Morning Music Ltd.
All Rights Reserved

English literal translation:

Verse 1:
When I'm alone,
I dream of the horizon
And words fail me.
There is no light
In a room where there is no sun.
And there is no sun if you're not here
With me, with me.
From every window,
Unfurl my heart,
The heart that you have won.
Into me you've poured the light,
The light that you've found
By the side of the road.

Chorus:
Time to say goodbye.
Places that I've never seen
Or experienced with you,
Now I shall.
I'll sail with you upon ships across the seas,
Seas that exist no more.
It's time to say goodbye.

Verse 2:
When you're far away,
I dream of the horizon
And words fail me.
And of course, I know that you're with me,
With me.
You, my moon, you are with me.
My sun, you're here with me,
With me, with me.

Chorus:
Time to say goodbye.
Places that I've never seen
Or experienced with you,
Now I shall.
I'll sail with you upon ships across the seas,
Seas that exist no more,
I'll revive them with you.

Tag:
I'll go with you upon ships across the seas,
Seas that exist no more,
I'll revive them with you.
I'll go with you,
I'll go with you.

UN-BREAK MY HEART

Words and Music by
DIANE WARREN
Arranged by DAN COATES

Un-Break My Heart - 5 - 1

© 1996, 1997 REALSONGS (ASCAP)
All Rights Reserved

Un-do___ this hurt you caused___ when you walked out the door___ and walked

out of my life.___ Un - cry___ these tears I

cried so man - y nights.___ Un - break___ my heart.___

UNTIL I FIND YOU AGAIN

Music and Lyrics by
RICHARD MARX
Arranged by DAN COATES

© 1997 CHI-BOY MUSIC
All Rights Reserved

VALENTINE

Composed by
JIM BRICKMAN and **JACK KUGELL**
Arranged by DAN COATES

© 1996 BRICKMAN ARRANGEMENT (SESAC)/EMI APRIL MUSIC INC./DOXIE MUSIC (ASCAP)
All Rights Reserved

Verse 2:
All of my life,
I have been waiting for all you give to me.
You've opened my eyes
And shown me how to love unselfishly.
I've dreamed of this a thousand times before,
But in my dreams I couldn't love you more.
I will give you my heart until the end of time.
You're all I need, my love,
My Valentine.

WHEREVER YOU GO

Words and Music by
DURELL BOTTOMS, NICOLE RENEE
and MICHAEL McCRARY
Arranged by DAN COATES

© 1998 WB MUSIC CORP., SURE II HIT MUSIC, MELODEUS FOOL MUSIC,
ENSIGN MUSIC CORPORATION, BLACK PANTHER PUBLISHING CO. and RARE BIRD PUBLISHING
All Rights on behalf of WB MUSIC CORP., SURE II HIT MUSIC and MELODEUS FOOL MUSIC Administered by WB MUSIC CORP.
All Rights Reserved

198

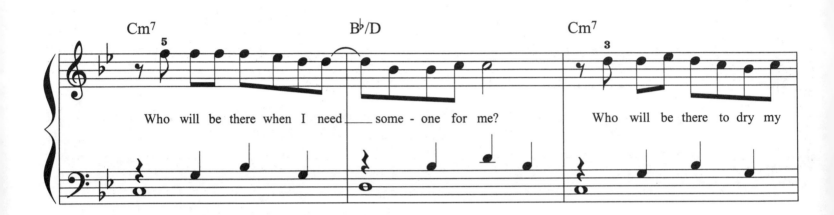

Verse 2:
Goodbye is such a hard thing to say
When you're all I know,
When you're my everything.
And who will stay and care for me?
When you're gone, I'll be all alone.
Who will come and comfort me
And fulfill my needs?
Who will love me?
Who will care?
Who will be there
When I need someone for me?
Who will be there to dry my eyes
When I go down on my knees?
I need you to say:
(To Chorus:)

YOU MEAN THE WORLD TO ME

Words and Music by
L.A. REID, DARYL SIMMONS
and BABYFACE
Arranged by DAN COATES

You Mean the World to Me - 6 - 1

© 1993, 1994 WARNER-TAMERLANE PUBLISHING CORP., BOOBIE-LOO MUSIC, STIFF SHIRT MUSIC, INC., SONY SONGS, INC. and ECAF MUSIC
All Rights on behalf of BOOBIE-LOO MUSIC and STIFF SHIRT MUSIC, INC. Administered by WARNER-TAMERLANE PUBLISHING CORP.
All Rights on behalf of SONY SONGS, INC. and ECAF Administered by SONY MUSIC PUBLISHING
All Rights Reserved

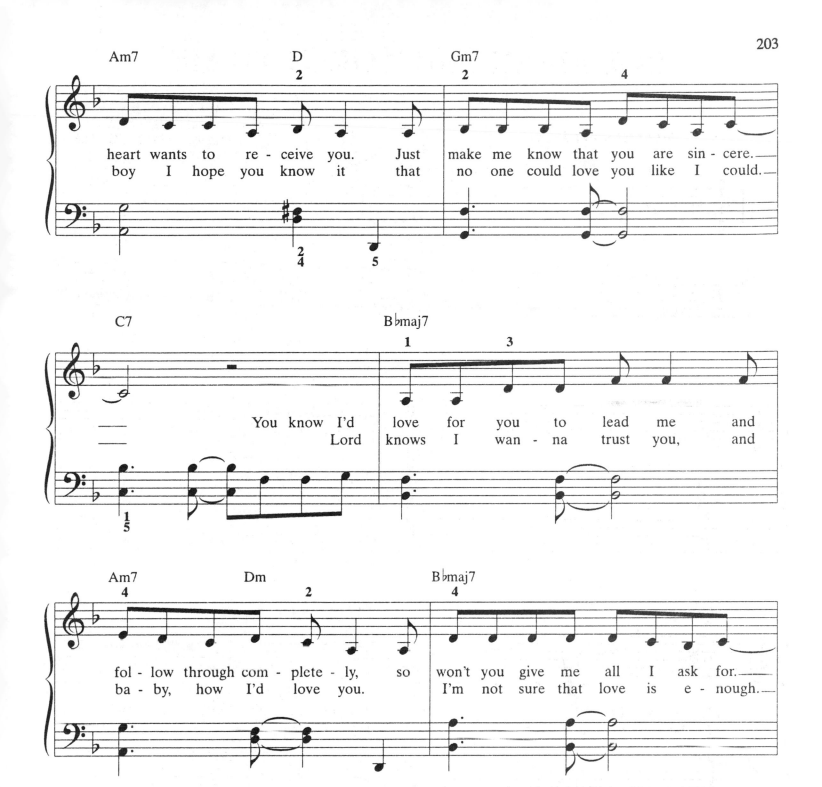

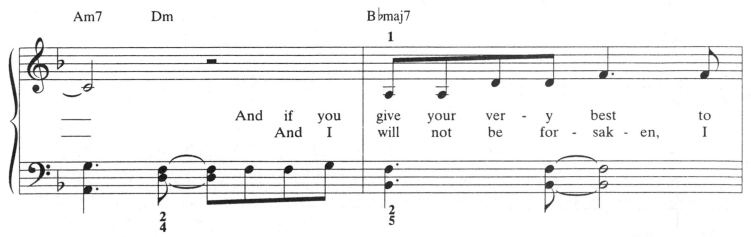

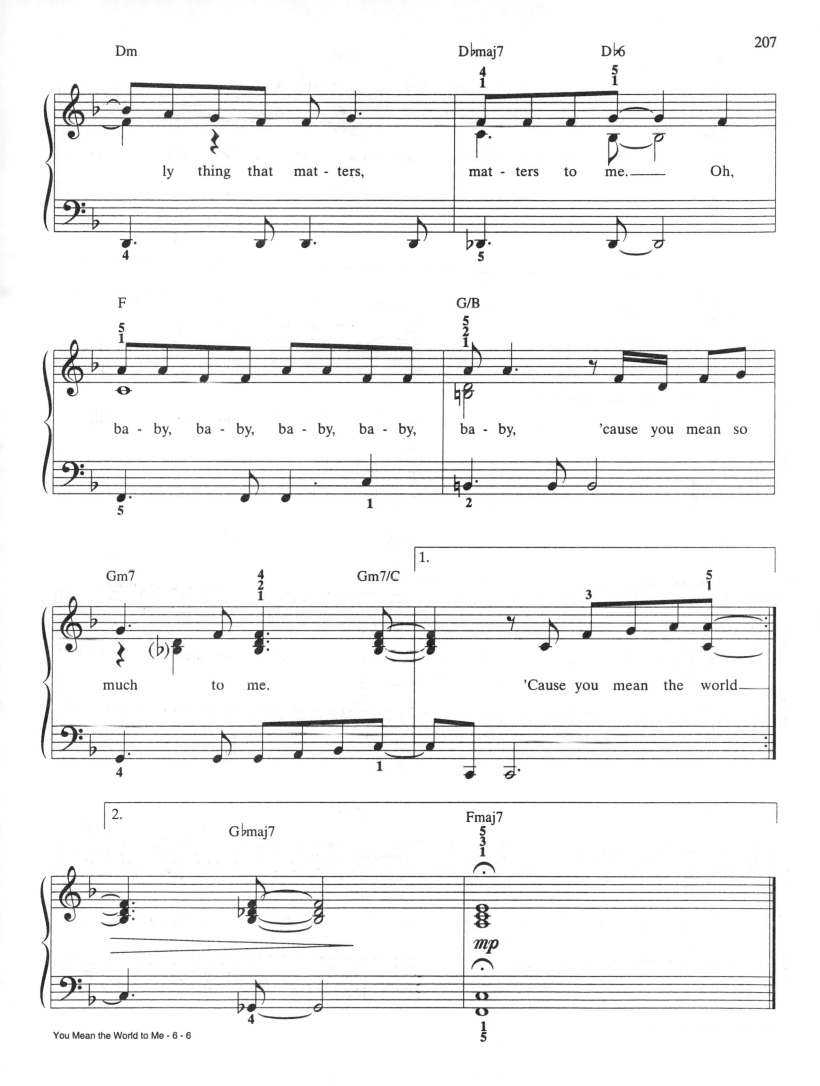

YOU WERE MEANT FOR ME

Words and Music by
JEWEL KILCHER and STEVE POLTZ
Arranged by DAN COATES

Moderate swing feel

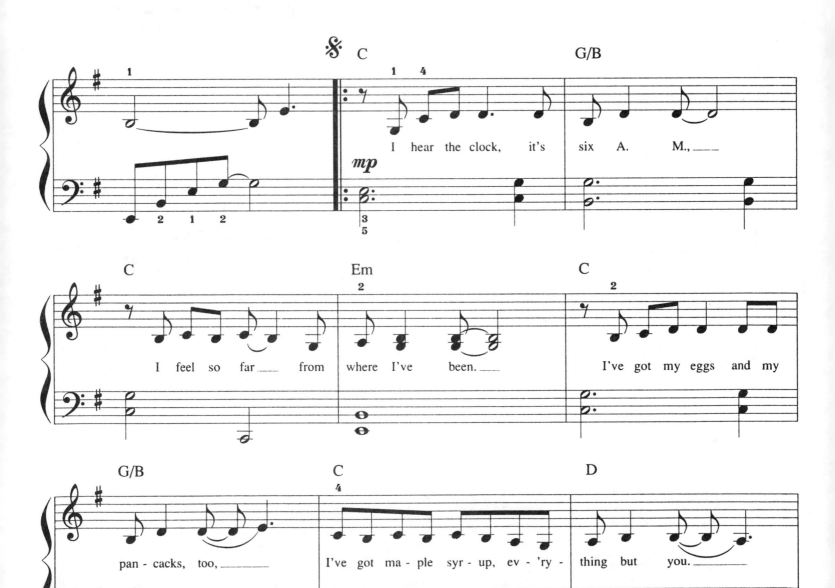

Lyrics:

I hear the clock, it's six A. M.,
I feel so far from where I've been.
I've got my eggs and my pan-cacks, too,
I've got ma-ple syr-up, ev-'ry-thing but you.

© 1995 WB MUSIC CORP., WIGGLY TOOTH MUSIC and POLIO BOY
This Arrangement © 1996 WB MUSIC CORP., WIGGLY TOOTH MUSIC and POLIO BOY
All Rights on behalf of WIGGLY TOOTH MUSIC Administered by WB MUSIC CORP.
All Rights Reserved

I break the yolks and make a smil-y face,_____ I kind of like it in my

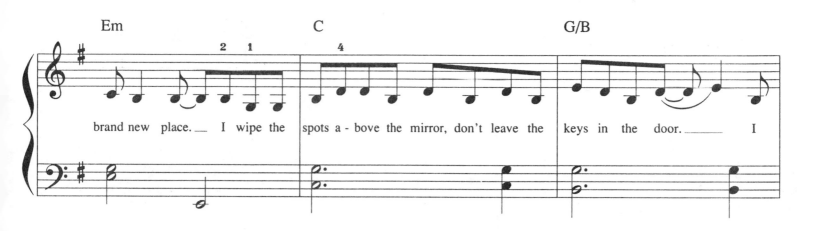

brand new place._ I wipe the spots a-bove the mirror, don't leave the keys in the door._____ I

nev-er put wet tow-els on the floor an-y-more,_ 'cause dreams_ last_ for
cresc.

so_____ long,_____ ev-en af-ter you're gone._____

You Were Meant for Me - 5 - 2

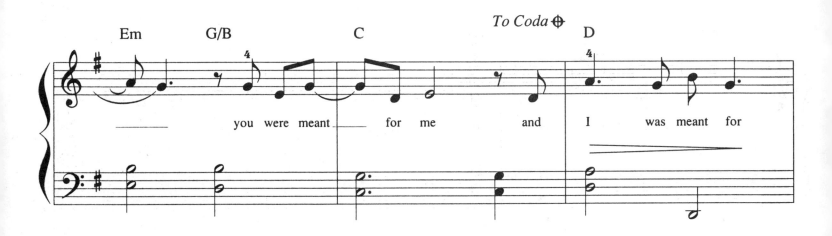

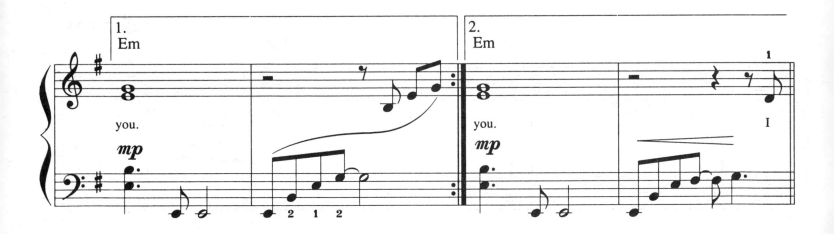

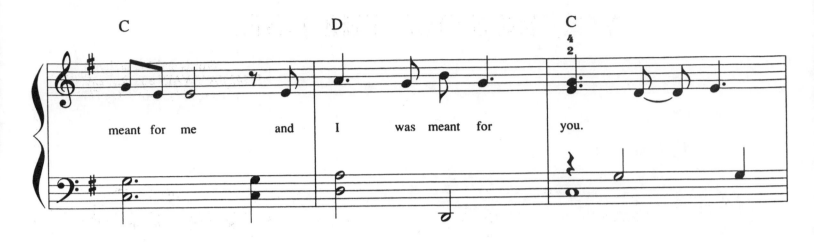

C   D   C

meant for me   and   I   was meant for   you.

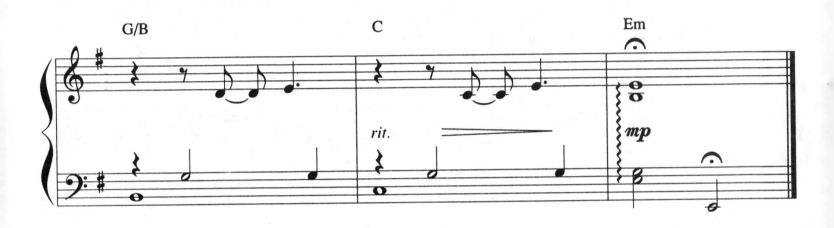

G/B   C   Em

rit.

mp

Verse 2:
I called my mama, she was out for a walk.
Consoled a cup of coffee, but it didn't wanna talk.
So I picked up a paper, it was more bad news,
More hearts being broken or people being used.
Put on my coat in the pouring rain.
I saw a movie, it just wasn't the same,
'Cause it was happy and I was sad,
And it made me miss you, oh, so bad.
(To Chorus:)

Verse 3:
I brush my teeth and put the cap back on,
I know you hate it when I leave the light on.
I pick a book up and then I turn the sheets down,
And then I take a breath and a good look around.
Put on my pj's and hop into bed.
I'm half alive but I feel mostly dead.
I try and tell myself it'll be all right,
I just shouldn't think anymore tonight.
(To Chorus:)

YOU'RE STILL THE ONE

Words and Music by
SHANIA TWAIN and R.J. LANGE
Arranged by DAN COATES

You're Still the One - 3 - 1

© 1997 SONGS OF POLYGRAM INT'L INC./LOON ECHO INC. (BMI); OUT OF POCKET PRODUCTIONS LTD.
All Rights on behalf of OUT OF POCKET PRODUCTIONS LTD. Controlled by ZOMBA ENTERPRISES INC. (ASCAP) for the U.S. and Canada
All Rights Reserved   Used by Permission   International Copyright Secured

DAN COATES

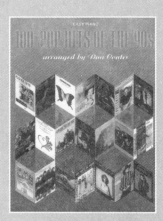

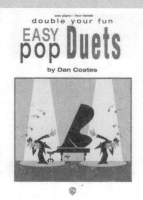
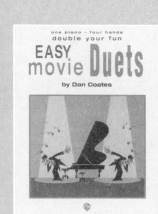

AD139   Printed in USA